Easy Microwave
Desserts in a Mug®
Third Edition

Gloria Hander Lyons

Blue Sage Press

Easy Microwave Desserts in a Mug®
Third Edition

Inquires should be addressed to:

Blue Sage Press
48 Borondo Pines
La Marque, TX 77568
www.BlueSagePress.com

ISBN: 978-0-9842438-1-5

Library of Congress Control Number: 2007900550

Third Edition: November 2009

Printed in the United States of America

Table of Contents

Breakfast Treat Mixes

Hot Beverage Mixes

Desserts-in-a-Mug Gift Ideas

Easy Microwave Desserts in a Mug®
Third Edition

General Information

Important—Don't Skip This Part!!

Quick and easy microwave desserts in a mug are the perfect solution for today's on-the-go families, singles, seniors, college dorm students and RV travelers. They are also handy if you want a late night snack for one, or a last-minute, "right-out-of-the-oven" breakfast treat.

For those of you who love to bake and enjoy homemade desserts, but need to watch your calorie intake, these single-serving portions will come to the rescue. You'll no longer be tempted to have a second or third serving.

The desserts-in-a-mug mixes also make fun cooking projects for kids, whether measuring the ingredients to make the mix or simply using the mix to prepare a treat. With a bit of adult supervision, each child can make his own special dessert.

These single-serving desserts are prepared, cooked and served in the same mug. Each mug mix includes all the ingredients you need to prepare your treat (including a single-serving size container of fruit or vegetables for some recipes). All you add is butter or margarine and/or water; and in five minutes or less, you have a tasty dessert, breakfast pastry or hot beverage.

You can stir up a mix any time you get the urge for a sweet treat, or make them ahead of time and store them in small plastic zipper-type bags to give as unique, inexpensive gifts or for your own use at a later date.

These tasty mug mixes are simple to make, cost less than store-bought mixes, and don't contain the preservatives found in many of the manufactured versions.

Since you prepare them yourself, you can adjust the ingredients to suit your own taste. If you or your family members have food allergies, such as wheat, eggs, milk or nuts, simply substitute special ingredients to meet your needs.

These treats are easy, quick and right-out-of-the-oven delicious! The hardest part about making them is waiting until they're cool enough to eat.

You'll want to try them all!

Mixing

This edition of *Easy Microwave Desserts in a Mug* includes mix recipes for more than 100 delectable desserts, breakfast treats and hot beverages—all in single-serving, easy to cook portions.

The most important thing to keep in mind when preparing small serving-size mixes is accuracy in measuring. All the amounts listed in each recipe are for level measurements for measuring spoons and cups. Keep a straight-edge utensil handy for this purpose.

Some of the recipes call for one-half of a tablespoon of ingredients. If you don't own a one-half tablespoon measure, it is equal to one and a half teaspoons.

* * * * * *

Helpful Hint: Before starting to mix your ingredients together, line up all the ingredients called for in the recipe (flour, sugar, salt, baking powder, egg white powder, etc.) on your counter. As you add each one, move it to another section of the counter or to a different counter, so you'll know it's already been added to the mix. This way, you won't forget to add an ingredient or accidentally add it twice!

* * * * * *

Note: Although most of these recipes call for butter or margarine, you may substitute a more heart-healthy butter-flavored spread, such as Smart Balance® or Promise®, which comes in easy-to-measure sticks. Just make sure the butter substitute you choose is meant for use in cooking.

3

Cooking

Make sure the mug you use for preparing the mixes is microwave safe, and that it will hold at *least* 12 ounces (or 1-1/2 cups) of liquid.

All the recipes in this book were tested in a 1000 Watt microwave oven. Since microwave wattages vary, you might need to make slight adjustments in cooking times and power settings for your oven.

Don't overcook your cakes and cookies or they will be tough and dry. A bit of moisture on the top after baking is normal. Test for doneness with a toothpick inserted into the cake if you aren't sure.

The cooking instructions for some of the mixes include covering the mug after cooking and letting the food stand in the microwave for a few minutes to finish the cooking process. I use a small plate or saucer for this purpose.

The handle of the mug doesn't usually get hot during cooking, but the outside of the mug will be very hot, so it's best to use a hot pad or oven mitt to remove it from the oven.

Important Note: If your microwave doesn't have a turntable, rotate the mug one quarter turn half-way through the cooking time for more even baking.

Special Ingredients

For greater ease in preparation, the dessert mixes that require the addition of eggs are made using egg white powder. Egg white powder (a well-known brand is called Just Whites®) can be found in most large supermarkets on the baking aisle. You can also use meringue powder which is found in the cake decorating section at most discount stores and craft stores. Using whole egg powder is fine, too, but it is not generally stocked in most grocery stores.

Some of the dry mix recipes call for vanilla powder, but this ingredient is optional. When preparing the dessert, you can substitute vanilla extract for the vanilla powder if you like, or simply omit it from the recipe. Vanilla powder is measured exactly the same as vanilla extract.

Vanilla powder is available in a few large grocery stores and gourmet stores, but you can order it and have it shipped directly to your door. It is more convenient to use than vanilla extract and adds extra flavor to the mixes.

To find ordering sources on-line, simply type "vanilla powder" into your search engine. I have listed a few sources below:

Barry Farm Enterprises   Cook's Flavoring Co.
419-228-4640   800-735-0545
www.barryfarm.com   www.cooksvanilla.com

San Francisco Herb Co.
800-227-4530 (For Orders)
www.sfherb.com

Another option for adding vanilla flavor to your dry mixes is to substitute vanilla sugar for the granulated or brown sugar called for in each recipe. See the recipes for making vanilla sugar on page 6.

Vanilla Sugar

If you don't want to purchase vanilla powder, another option for adding vanilla flavor to the desserts-in-a-mug mixes is to substitute the same amount of vanilla sugar for the granulated sugar or brown sugar called for in each recipe.

Use the recipes below to make your own vanilla sugar.

Vanilla-Flavored Granulated Sugar

To make your own vanilla sugar, mix 1 cup of granulated sugar with 1/2 teaspoon of vanilla extract. Stir until thoroughly blended. Spread in a shallow pan and let dry for 2-3 hours. Stir again to break up any lumps and store in an airtight container. Substitute this mixture for the amount of granulated sugar called for in each recipe.

Vanilla-Flavored Brown Sugar

To make vanilla-flavored brown sugar, blend 1 cup of firmly packed brown sugar with 1/2 teaspoon of vanilla extract. Stir until thoroughly blended and store in an air-tight container. Substitute this mixture for the amount of brown sugar called for in each recipe.

Packaging

If you're preparing the desserts-in-a-mug mixes to give as gifts or making them ahead of time for your own use at a later date, store them in small zipper-type plastic bags.

Sandwich-size bags (6-1/2" X 5-7/8") work well for the mixes that measure about 1/2 cup.

For the cake toppings (or other ingredients added separately) that measure about 1-2 tablespoons or less, use a double layer of plastic wrap, cut into a 4" or 5" square. Place the topping in the center of the plastic wrap, gather the corners together and secure with a twist tie.

Whether you're making these mixes to give away as one-of-a-kind gifts or for your own convenience, they will be welcome additions to the pantry.

Gift Ideas

These convenient single-serving mixes make unique, inexpensive gifts. Refer to the section called *"Desserts-in-a-Mug Gift Ideas"*, on page 105, for creative gift-giving suggestions. There you'll find instructions for making attractive mix-in-a-mug gifts for various occasions.

Simply line a mug with colorful tissue paper and place a bag of mix inside. Then write the cooking instructions on a small tag and attach to the mug handle, using colorful ribbon, or write them on a recipe card and tuck inside the mug.

A few of the fun ideas listed are: "Birthday Cake in a Mug", "Thanks a Latte" and "You're a Peach!"

This section also includes instructions for putting together creative gift baskets, such as: "Coffee Lover's" gift basket and "Afternoon Tea Party" gift basket.

Surprise a friend or family member with a "one-of-a-kind" gift that you made yourself!

Dessert Mixes

Brownies & Cookies

Coconut Pecan Blondie Mix

1/4 cup flour
1/4 cup brown sugar, packed
1-1/2 tablespoons sweetened flaked coconut, firmly packed
1 tablespoon finely chopped pecans
1 teaspoon egg white powder
1/4 teaspoon vanilla powder* (optional)
1/8 teaspoon baking powder
Dash of salt

Blend ingredients together and place in a small zipper-type bag if using at a later date or giving as a gift.

To prepare: Microwave 1-1/2 tablespoons butter or margarine in mug until melted. Empty cookie mix into mug and add 1-1/2 tablespoons water; stirring with a fork until blended. Microwave on 60% power for 2 minutes. Let stand in the microwave 2 minutes. Remove from oven and let stand until cool enough to eat.

*If you don't have vanilla powder, stir 1/4 teaspoon vanilla extract into mix when adding water or substitute vanilla-flavored brown sugar for brown sugar in recipe (vanilla sugar recipes on page 6).

Chocolate Brownie Mix

1/4 cup granulated sugar
3 tablespoons flour
2 tablespoons semi-sweet chocolate chips (mini chips are best)
1 tablespoon unsweetened cocoa
1 tablespoon finely chopped pecans (optional)
1-1/2 teaspoons egg white powder
1/4 teaspoon vanilla powder* (optional)
1/8 teaspoon baking powder
Dash of salt

Blend ingredients together and place in a small zipper-type bag if using at a later date or giving as a gift.

To prepare: Microwave 1-1/2 tablespoons butter or margarine in mug until melted (about 20 seconds on high power). Empty brownie mix into mug and add 2 tablespoons water; stirring with a fork until blended.

Microwave on 60% power for 2 minutes. Let stand in oven 2 minutes. Do not over bake or the brownie will be dry. A bit of moisture on top is normal after baking. Remove mug from oven and let stand until brownie is cool enough to eat.

*If you don't have vanilla powder, stir 1/8 teaspoon vanilla extract into mix when adding water or substitute vanilla sugar for granulated sugar (vanilla sugar recipe on page 6).

Mocha Brownie Mix

Add 1/4 teaspoon instant coffee granules to the Chocolate Brownie Mix recipe. Prepare as directed for Chocolate Brownie Mix.

Chocolate Mint Brownie Mix

Substitute 2 tablespoons of mint chocolate chips for the semi-sweet chocolate chips in the Chocolate Brownie Mix recipe. Prepare as directed for Chocolate Brownie Mix.

Chocolate Cherry Brownie Mix

Substitute 1 tablespoon of finely chopped dried cherries for the chopped pecans in the Chocolate Brownie Mix recipe. Prepare as directed for Chocolate Brownie Mix. (Optional: Let batter stand 5 minutes before cooking to partially rehydrate fruit if desired.)

Almond Joy Brownie Mix

Substitute 1 tablespoon of finely chopped almonds for the chopped pecans in the Chocolate Brownie Mix recipe and add 1 tablespoon of firmly packed, sweetened, flaked coconut. Prepare as directed for Chocolate Brownie Mix.

Chocolate Chip Cookie Mix

3 tablespoons flour
3 tablespoons semi-sweet chocolate chips (mini chips are best)
1-1/2 tablespoons brown sugar, firmly packed
1 tablespoon granulated sugar
1 tablespoon finely chopped pecans
1 teaspoon egg white powder
1/4 teaspoon vanilla powder (optional)
1/8 teaspoon baking soda
Dash of salt

Blend ingredients together and place in a small zipper-type bag if using at a later date or giving as a gift.

To prepare: Microwave 1-1/2 tablespoons butter or margarine in mug until melted (about 20 seconds on high power).

Empty mix into mug and add 1-1/2 tablespoons water; stirring with a fork until blended. Microwave on 60% power for 2 minutes. Let stand in microwave 2 minutes. Remove and let stand until cool enough to eat.

Oatmeal Raisin Cookie Mix

2 tablespoons quick cooking oats
1-1/2 tablespoons flour
1-1/2 tablespoons brown sugar, firmly packed
1 tablespoon granulated sugar
1 tablespoon raisins
1 teaspoon egg white powder
1/8 teaspoon baking soda
1/8 teaspoon ground cinnamon
1/8 teaspoon vanilla powder (optional)
Dash of salt

Blend ingredients together and place in a small zipper-type bag if using at a later date or giving as a gift.

To prepare: Microwave 1-1/2 tablespoons butter or margarine in mug until melted (20 seconds on high power).

Empty mix into mug and add 1-1/2 tablespoons water; stirring with a fork until blended. Microwave on 60% power for 2 minutes. Let stand in microwave 2 minutes. Remove from oven and let stand until cool enough to eat.

Peanut Butter Cookie Mix

3 tablespoons flour
1 tablespoon brown sugar, firmly packed
1 tablespoon granulated sugar
1 teaspoon egg white powder
1/8 teaspoon vanilla powder (optional)
1/8 teaspoon baking soda
Dash of salt

Blend ingredients together and place in a small zipper-type bag if using at a later date or giving as a gift.

Additional Ingredients:

Measure into a separate small bag or wrap in plastic wrap:
3 tablespoons peanut butter baking chips

To prepare: Place 1-1/2 tablespoons butter or margarine and peanut butter chips in mug. Microwave until butter is melted (about 20 seconds on high power). Stir until chips are melted.

Empty mix into mug and add 1-1/2 tablespoons water; stirring with a fork until blended.

Microwave on 60% power for 2 minutes. Let stand in microwave 2 minutes. Remove and let stand until cool enough to eat.

Cowboy Cookie Mix

2 tablespoons flour
1-1/2 tablespoons quick cooking oats
1 tablespoon semi-sweet chocolate chips (mini chips are best)
1 tablespoon finely chopped pecans
1 tablespoon sweetened, flaked coconut, firmly packed
1-1/2 tablespoons brown sugar, firmly packed
1 tablespoon granulated sugar
1 teaspoon egg white powder
1/8 teaspoon vanilla powder (optional)
1/8 teaspoon baking soda
Dash of salt

Blend ingredients together and place in a small zipper-type bag if using at a later date or giving as a gift.

To prepare: Microwave 1-1/2 tablespoons butter or margarine in mug until melted (about 20 seconds on high power).

Empty mix into mug and add 1-1/2 tablespoons water; stirring with a fork until blended.

Microwave on 60% power for 2 minutes. Let stand in microwave 2 minutes. Remove and let stand until cool enough to eat.

S'mores Mix

1/2 cup of coarsely crushed graham crackers
1/2 cup of miniature marshmallows
1/4 cup of semi-sweet or milk chocolate chips

Combine all ingredients and place in a zipper-type bag if using at a later date or giving as a gift.

To prepare: Empty mix into mug.

Microwave on high power for 30-45 seconds, or until marshmallows are puffed and melted.

Let stand in microwave 2 minutes to soften chocolate chips. Enjoy.

Rice Crispy Treat Mix

1/4 cup mini marshmallows
1 tablespoon peanut butter baking chips

Combine ingredients and place in a small zipper-type bag if using at a later date or giving as a gift.

Additional Ingredients:

Measure into a separate small bag:
        1/3 cup Rice Crispy cereal

To prepare: Microwave 1/2 tablespoon margarine in mug on high power until melted.

Stir in marshmallows and peanut butter chips. Microwave on high power 15-20 seconds until just beginning to melt.

Stir mixture until smooth and well blended. Add cereal and stir until blended. Let stand until cool enough to eat.

Dessert Mixes

Cakes

Yellow Cake Mix
(Try a Birthday Cake in a Mug)

1/4 cup flour
3 tablespoons granulated
  sugar
1 tablespoon instant nonfat
  dry milk
1 teaspoon egg white powder
1/4 teaspoon baking powder
1/8 teaspoon vanilla powder
  (optional—see page 6)
Dash of salt

Blend ingredients together and place in a small zipper-type bag if using at a later date or giving as a gift.

Chocolate Buttercream Frosting Mix
In a separate small zipper-type bag, combine the following ingredients: 1/3 cup powdered sugar
  1-1/2 teaspoons unsweetened cocoa
  1 teaspoon instant nonfat dry milk

To prepare cake: Microwave 1-1/2 tablespoons butter or margarine in mug until melted (about 20 seconds on high power). Empty cake mix into mug and add 3 tablespoons water; stirring with a fork until blended. Microwave on 60% power for 2 minutes. Let stand in oven 2 minutes. Remove and let stand until cool enough to frost.

To make frosting: Add 1 teaspoon butter or margarine and 1 teaspoon water to frosting mix in zipper-type bag. Close and gently rub bag until frosting is smooth. Add more water if frosting is too dry. Squeeze frosting down into one corner of bag and cut off tip of corner. Squeeze frosting out onto warm cake. –OR- Mix frosting in a small bowl and spread on warm cake.

Pineapple Right-side Up Cake Mix

1/4 cup flour
3 tablespoons granulated sugar
1 tablespoon instant nonfat dry milk
1 teaspoon egg white powder
1/4 teaspoon baking powder
1/8 teaspoon vanilla powder
    (optional—see page 6)
Dash of salt

Blend ingredients together and place in a small zipper-type bag if using at a later date or giving as a gift.

Topping mix:
In a separate small zipper-type bag or plastic wrap, combine the following ingredients:
        2 teaspoons brown sugar, packed
        1/8 teaspoon ground cinnamon

Additional ingredients:
1 (4 ounce) snack size container of pineapple tidbits

To prepare: Microwave 1-1/2 tablespoons butter or margarine in mug until melted. Empty cake mix into mug and add 3 tablespoons water; stirring with a fork until blended.

Drain juice from pineapple. Stir one tablespoon of tidbits into batter. Carefully place about 2 tablespoons of tidbits on top of the cake batter in a single layer (discard remaining pineapple or save for another use). Sprinkle with topping mix.

Microwave on 60% power for 2-1/2 minutes. Let stand in microwave 2 minutes. Remove from oven and let stand until cool enough to eat.

Chocolate Cake Mix

3 tablespoons flour
3 tablespoons granulated sugar
1 tablespoon unsweetened cocoa powder
1 tablespoon instant nonfat dry milk
1 teaspoon egg white powder
1/4 teaspoon baking powder
1/8 teaspoon vanilla powder (optional—see page 6)
Dash of salt

Blend ingredients together and place in a small zipper-type bag if using at a later date or giving as a gift.

Chocolate Buttercream Frosting Mix

In a separate small zipper-type bag, combine the following ingredients:

    1/3 cup powdered sugar
    1-1/2 teaspoons unsweetened cocoa powder
    1 teaspoon instant nonfat dry milk

To prepare cake: Microwave 1-1/2 tablespoons butter or margarine in mug until melted (about 20 seconds on high power). Empty cake mix into mug and add 3 tablespoons water; stirring with a fork until blended. Microwave on 60% power for 2 minutes. Let stand in oven for 2 minutes. Remove and let stand until cool enough to frost.

To make frosting: Add 1 teaspoon butter or margarine and 1 teaspoon water to frosting mix in zipper-type bag. Close and gently rub bag until frosting is smooth. Add more water if frosting is too dry. Squeeze frosting down into one corner of bag and cut off tip of corner. Squeeze onto warm cake. –OR– Mix frosting in a small bowl and spread on warm cake.

Carrot Cake Mix

1/4 cup flour
3 tablespoons granulated sugar
1 tablespoon finely chopped pecans
1 teaspoon egg white powder
1/4 teaspoon baking powder
1/4 teaspoon ground cinnamon
1/8 teaspoon vanilla powder (optional—see page 6)
1/16 teaspoon ground nutmeg
Dash of salt

Blend ingredients together and place in a zipper-type bag if using at a later date or giving as a gift.

Additional ingredients:
1 (2.5 ounce) jar of strained carrots (baby food)

Vanilla Buttercream Frosting Mix
In a separate small zipper-type bag, combine the following ingredients: 1/3 cup powdered sugar
1 teaspoon instant nonfat dry milk
1/8 teaspoon vanilla powder (optional)

To prepare cake: Microwave 1-1/2 tablespoons butter or margarine in mug until melted. Stir 2 tablespoons of carrots into mug. Empty cake mix into mug and add 1 tablespoon water; stirring with a fork until blended. Microwave on 60% power for 2-1/2 minutes. Let stand in microwave for 2 minutes. Remove and let stand until cool enough to frost.

To make frosting: Add 1 teaspoon butter or margarine and 1 teaspoon water to frosting mix in zipper-type bag. Close and gently rub bag until frosting is smooth. Add more water if frosting is too dry. Squeeze frosting down into one corner of bag and cut off tip of corner. Squeeze onto warm cake. -OR- Mix frosting in a small bowl and spread on warm cake.

German Chocolate Cake Mix

3 tablespoons flour
3 tablespoons granulated sugar
1 tablespoon unsweetened cocoa
1 tablespoon instant nonfat dry milk
1 tablespoon sweetened flaked coconut,
    firmly packed
1 tablespoon finely chopped pecans
1 teaspoon egg white powder
1/4 teaspoon baking powder
1/8 teaspoon vanilla powder (optional—see page 6)
Dash of salt

Blend ingredients together and place in a small zipper-type bag if using at a later date or giving as a gift.

Chocolate Glaze Mix
In a separate small zipper-type bag, combine the following ingredients:
    1/3 cup powdered sugar
    1-1/2 teaspoons unsweetened cocoa powder

To prepare cake: Microwave 1-1/2 tablespoons butter or margarine in mug until melted. Empty cake mix into mug and add 3 tablespoons water; stirring with a fork until blended. Microwave on 60% power for 2 minutes. Let stand in oven 2 minutes. Let cool slightly before adding glaze.

To make glaze: Add 1-1/2 teaspoons water to glaze mix in zipper-type bag. Close and rub bag until glaze is smooth. Cut off one bottom corner of glaze mix bag and apply glaze to warm cake. –OR- Mix glaze in a small bowl and pour on top of cake. Let cake stand until cool enough to eat.

Chocolate Cherry Nut Cake Mix

1/4 cup flour
2 tablespoons granulated sugar
2 tablespoons dried cherries, chopped
1 tablespoon finely chopped pecans
1 tablespoon semi-sweet chocolate chips
    (mini chips are best)
1 teaspoon egg white powder
1/4 teaspoon vanilla powder (optional—see page 6)
1/4 teaspoon baking powder
1/8 teaspoon ground cinnamon
Dash of salt

Blend ingredients together and place in a zipper-type bag if using at a later date or giving as a gift.

Chocolate Glaze Mix
In a separate small zipper-type bag, combine the following ingredients:
    1/3 cup powdered sugar
    1-1/2 teaspoons cocoa powder

To prepare cake: Microwave 1-1/2 tablespoons butter or margarine in mug until melted (about 20 seconds on high power). Empty cake mix into mug and add 3 tablespoons water; stirring with a fork until blended. (Optional: Let batter stand 5 minutes before cooking to partially rehydrate fruit if desired.) Microwave on 60% power for 2 minutes. Let stand in oven 2 minutes. Let cool slightly before adding glaze.

To make glaze: Add 1-1/2 teaspoons water to glaze mix in zipper-type bag. Close and rub bag until glaze is smooth. Cut off one bottom corner of glaze mix bag and apply glaze to warm cake. –OR- Mix glaze in a small bowl and pour on top of cake. Let cake stand until cool enough to eat.

Spiced Applesauce Cake Mix

1/4 cup flour
3 tablespoons brown sugar, firmly packed
1 tablespoon finely chopped walnuts
1 teaspoon egg white powder
1/4 teaspoon baking powder
1/8 teaspoon ground cinnamon
1/16 teaspoon ground ginger
1/16 teaspoon ground cloves
Dash of salt

Blend ingredients and place in a small zipper-type bag if using at a later date or giving as a gift.

Additional ingredients:
1 (2.5 ounce) jar of applesauce (baby food)

Cinnamon Glaze Mix
In a separate small zipper-type bag, combine the following ingredients: 1/3 cup powdered sugar
1/16 teaspoon ground cinnamon

To prepare cake: Microwave 1 tablespoon butter or margarine in mug until melted (about 20 seconds on high power). Stir 2 tablespoons of applesauce into mug. Empty cake mix into mug and add 1-1/2 tablespoons water; stirring with a fork until blended. Microwave on 60% power for 2-1/2 minutes. Let stand in oven 2 minutes. Remove and let cool slightly before adding glaze.

To make glaze: Add 1-1/2 teaspoons water to glaze mix in zipper-type bag. Close and rub bag until glaze is smooth. Cut off one bottom corner of glaze mix bag and apply glaze to warm cake. –OR- Mix glaze in a small bowl and pour on top of cake. Let cake stand until cool enough to eat.

Hot Fudge Cake Mix

As this cake bakes, it forms its own fudge sauce on the bottom. For an extra tasty treat, add a scoop of ice cream on top.

3 tablespoons flour
3 tablespoons granulated sugar
2 tablespoons finely chopped pecans
1 tablespoon instant nonfat dry milk
1/2 tablespoon unsweetened cocoa
1/8 teaspoon baking powder
1/4 teaspoon vanilla powder
   (optional—see page 6)
Dash of salt

Blend ingredients together and place in a zipper-type bag if using at a later date or giving as a gift.

Topping Mix:

Blend together and place in a separate small zipper-type bag or plastic wrap the following:
   2 tablespoons of brown sugar, packed
   1/2 tablespoon unsweetened cocoa powder

To prepare: Microwave 1 tablespoon butter or margarine in mug until melted (about 20 seconds on high power).

Empty cake mix into mug and add 2 tablespoons of water; stirring with a fork until blended. Sprinkle topping mix on top of batter. Pour 2 tablespoons water over topping, but do not stir.

Microwave on 60% power for 2 minutes. Let stand in oven 2 minutes. Remove and let stand until cool enough to eat.

Sugar Plum Cake Mix

1/4 cup flour
3 tablespoons granulated sugar
1 tablespoon instant nonfat dry milk
1 tablespoon finely chopped pecans
1 teaspoon egg white powder
1/4 teaspoon baking powder
1/8 teaspoon ground cinnamon
1/16 teaspoon ground nutmeg
Dash of salt

Blend ingredients together. Place in a small zipper-type bag if using at a later date or giving as a gift.

Additional ingredients:
One (2.5 ounce) jar of pureed plums or prunes (baby food)

Glaze Mix:
In a separate small zipper-type bag, place 1/3 cup powdered sugar.

To prepare cake: Microwave 1 tablespoon butter or margarine in mug until melted (about 20 seconds on high power). Stir 2 tablespoons of plums into mug. Empty cake mix into mug and add 1-1/2 tablespoons water; stirring with a fork until blended. Microwave on 60% power for 2-1/2 minutes. Let stand in oven 2 minutes. Remove from oven and let cool slightly before adding glaze.

To make glaze: Add 2 teaspoons plums to powdered sugar in zipper-type bag. Close and rub bag until glaze is smooth. Cut off one bottom corner of glaze mix bag and apply glaze to warm cake. –OR– Mix glaze in a small bowl and pour on top of cake. Let cake stand until cool enough to eat.

Italian Cream Cake Mix

1/4 cup flour
3 tablespoons granulated sugar
2 tablespoons firmly packed, sweetened flaked coconut
1 tablespoon finely chopped pecans
1 tablespoon instant nonfat dry milk
1 teaspoon egg white powder
1/4 teaspoon baking powder
1/8 teaspoon vanilla powder (optional—see page 6)
Dash of salt

Blend ingredients together and place in a small zipper-type bag if using at a later date or giving as a gift.

Coconut Pecan Frosting Mix
In a separate small zipper-type bag, combine the following ingredients: 1/3 cup powdered sugar
2 teaspoons firmly packed, flaked coconut
2 teaspoons finely chopped pecans
1 teaspoon instant nonfat dry milk
1/8 teaspoon vanilla powder (optional)

To prepare cake: Microwave 1-1/2 tablespoons butter or margarine in mug until melted (about 20 seconds on high power). Empty cake mix into mug and add 3 tablespoons water; stirring with a fork until blended. Microwave on 60% power for 2 minutes. Let stand in oven 2 minutes. Remove and let stand until cool enough to frost.

To make frosting: Add 1 teaspoon butter or margarine and 1 teaspoon water to frosting mix in zipper-type bag. Close and gently rub bag until frosting is smooth. Add more water if frosting is too dry. Squeeze frosting down into one corner of bag and cut off tip of corner. Squeeze frosting out onto warm cake. –OR- Mix frosting in a small bowl and spread on warm cake.

Lemon Cake Mix

1/4 cup flour
3 tablespoons granulated sugar
1 tablespoon instant nonfat dry milk
1 teaspoon egg white powder
1 teaspoon presweetened lemonade
   mix
1/4 teaspoon baking powder
1/4 teaspoon dried grated lemon peel
Dash of salt

Blend ingredients together and place in a small zipper-type bag if using at a later date or giving as a gift.

Lemon Buttercream Frosting Mix
In a separate small zipper-type bag, combine the following ingredients:
   1/3 cup powdered sugar
   1 teaspoon presweetened lemonade mix
   1 teaspoon instant nonfat dry milk

To prepare cake: Microwave 1-1/2 tablespoons butter or margarine in mug until melted (about 20 seconds on high power). Empty cake mix into mug and add 3 tablespoons water; stirring with a fork until blended. Microwave on 60% power for 2 minutes. Let stand in oven for 2 minutes. Remove and let stand until cool enough to frost.

To make frosting: Add 1 teaspoon butter or margarine and 1 teaspoon water to frosting mix in zipper-type bag. Close and gently rub bag until frosting is smooth. Add more water if frosting is too dry. Squeeze frosting down into one corner of bag and cut off tip of corner. Squeeze onto warm cake. –OR– Mix frosting in a small bowl and spread on warm cake.

Dessert Mixes
Candy & Fudge

Chocolate Fudge Mix

1/4 cup semi-sweet chocolate chips (mini chips are best)
1/4 teaspoon vanilla powder (optional)
1 tablespoon finely chopped pecans

Blend ingredients together and place in a small zipper-type bag if using at a later date or giving as a gift.

Measure into a separate small zipper-type bag:
    1/3 cup mini marshmallows

To prepare: Microwave 1 tablespoon margarine in mug on high power 20 seconds until melted.

Stir in fudge mix and microwave on high power 15-20 seconds until just beginning to melt. *Do not allow mixture to boil.*

Stir in marshmallows and microwave for another 10-15 seconds until marshmallows are puffed and melted. Stir mixture until smooth and well blended.

Let stand until cool enough to eat or place mug in refrigerator for about 20 minutes until fudge sets.

Peanut Butter Chocolate Fudge Mix

Reduce the amount of semi-sweet chocolate chips in the Chocolate Fudge Mix recipe to 2 tablespoons and add 2 tablespoons of peanut butter baking chips. Omit nuts and vanilla powder. Prepare as directed for Chocolate Fudge Mix.

Chocolate Mint Fudge Mix

Substitute 1/4 cup of mint chocolate chips for the semi-sweet chocolate chips in the Chocolate Fudge Mix recipe. Omit nuts and vanilla powder. Prepare as directed for Chocolate Fudge Mix.

Chocolate Covered Cherry Fudge Mix

Substitute 1 tablespoon of finely chopped dried cherries for the pecans in the Chocolate Fudge Mix recipe. Prepare as directed for Chocolate Fudge Mix.

Chocolate Oatmeal Candy Mix

3 tablespoons granulated sugar
1/2 tablespoon instant nonfat dry milk
2 teaspoons unsweetened cocoa powder
1/8 teaspoon vanilla powder* (optional)
Dash of salt

Blend ingredients together and place in a small zipper-type bag if using at a later date or giving as a gift.

Measure into a separate small zipper-type bag:
    3 tablespoons quick cooking oatmeal (not instant)
    1-1/2 tablespoons sweetened, flaked coconut

To prepare: Microwave 1 tablespoon butter or margarine in mug until melted (about 20 seconds on high power).

Empty candy mix into mug and add 1-1/2 tablespoons of water; stirring with a fork until blended.

Microwave on high power 2-1/2 minutes; stirring after each 30-40 seconds, until thickened. Stir in oatmeal and coconut until well blended. Let stand until cool enough to eat.

*If you don't have vanilla powder, stir 1/8 teaspoon vanilla extract into candy mix when adding water or substitute vanilla sugar for granulated sugar (vanilla sugar recipe is on page 6).

Cranberry Cashew Candy Mix

1-1/2 tablespoons dried cranberries, finely chopped
1 tablespoon chopped cashews
1/4 cup mini marshmallows

Blend ingredients and place in a small zipper-type bag if using at a later date or giving as a gift.

Measure into a separate small zipper-type bag:

    1/4 cup white chocolate chips

To prepare: Microwave 1/2 tablespoon margarine in mug on high power (about 10 seconds on high power) until melted.

Stir in white chocolate chips and microwave on high power 15-20 seconds until just beginning to melt. Stir mixture until smooth. Stir in candy mix.

Microwave on high power 15-20 seconds until marshmallows are puffed and melted. Stir until well blended.

Let stand until cool enough to eat or place mug in refrigerator for about 20 minutes until candy sets.

Butterscotch Peanut Candy Mix

2 tablespoons butterscotch baking chips
2 tablespoons peanut butter baking chips
1 tablespoon finely chopped peanuts

Blend ingredients together and place in a small zipper-type bag if using at a later date or giving as a gift.

Measure into a separate small zipper-type bag:

1/3 cup mini marshmallows

To prepare: Microwave 1 tablespoon margarine in mug on high power about 20 seconds or until melted.

Stir in candy mix and microwave on high power 15-20 seconds until just beginning to melt. *Do not allow mixture to boil.*

Stir in marshmallows and microwave for another 15-20 seconds until marshmallows are puffed and melted. Stir mixture until smooth and well blended.

Let stand until cool enough to eat or place mug in refrigerator for about 20 minutes until candy sets.

Cow Pie Candy Mix

1 tablespoon raisins (or dried fruit of your choice, chopped)
1 tablespoon slivered almonds, chopped
1 tablespoon sweetened, flaked coconut, firmly packed

Blend ingredients and place in a small zipper-type bag if using at a later date or giving as a gift.

Measure into a separate small zipper-type bag:

1/4 cup semi-sweet chocolate chips
(mini chips are best)

To prepare: Place chocolate chips in mug and microwave on high power 15-20 seconds until just beginning to melt.

Stir mixture until smooth. Microwave an additional 10-15 seconds if needed. Stir in candy mix.

Let stand until cool enough to eat or place mug in refrigerator for about 20 minutes until candy sets.

Chocolate Chow Candy Mix

2 tablespoons chow mein noodles, coarsely crushed
1 tablespoon roasted peanuts, chopped
1 tablespoon finely chopped, dried dates (or dried fruit of
   your choice)

Blend ingredients and place in a small zipper-type bag if using
at a later date or giving as a gift.

Measure into a separate small zipper-type bag:

> 2 tablespoons semi-sweet chocolate chips
> 2 tablespoons butterscotch (or peanut butter) baking
>   chips

To prepare: Place chocolate chips and butterscotch baking
chips in mug and microwave on high power 15-20 seconds
until just beginning to melt. Stir mixture until smooth.
Microwave an additional 10-15 seconds if needed. Stir in
candy mix.

Let stand until cool enough to eat or place mug in refrigerator
for about 20 minutes until candy sets.

Dessert Mixes

Pies, Cobblers & Crisps

Apple Pie Mix

2 tablespoons flour
1 tablespoon instant nonfat dry milk
1 tablespoon granulated sugar
1 teaspoon egg white powder
1/16 teaspoon baking powder
1/8 teaspoon ground cinnamon
Dash of salt

Blend all ingredients and place in a small zipper-type bag if using at a later date or giving as a gift.

In a separate zipper-type bag, place:
    1/4 cup finely chopped dried apples

Topping Mix:
In a small zipper-type bag or plastic wrap, combine the following ingredients:
    2 teaspoons brown sugar, firmly packed
    1 teaspoon finely chopped pecans
    1/16 teaspoon ground cinnamon

To prepare: Place apples in mug and add 3 tablespoons water. Microwave on high power 1 minute or until boiling. Cover and let stand in the oven 5 minutes.

Remove from oven and stir in 1/2 tablespoon butter or margarine until melted.

Empty pie mix into mug and add 2 tablespoons water. Stir with a fork until well blended. Sprinkle topping mix on top of batter.

Microwave on 60% power for 2 minutes. Let stand in microwave 2 minutes. Remove and let stand until cool enough to eat.

Chocolate Cream Pie Mix

2-1/2 tablespoons granulated sugar
1 tablespoon flour
1 tablespoon instant nonfat dry milk
1-1/2 teaspoons egg white powder
1/8 teaspoon vanilla powder* (optional)
1/16 teaspoon baking powder
Dash of salt

Blend all ingredients together and place in a small zipper-type bag if using at a later date or giving as a gift.

Additional Ingredients:
In a separate zipper-type bag, place 2 tablespoons semi-sweet chocolate chips (mini-size morsels are easier to measure).

To prepare: Place chocolate chips and 1 tablespoon of butter in mug. Microwave on high power until butter is melted (about 20-30 seconds on high power). Stir until chocolate is melted.

Empty mix into mug and add 2-1/2 tablespoons of water. Stir with a fork until well blended. Microwave on 60% power for 2 minutes. Let stand in the microwave 2 minutes. Remove and let stand until cool enough to eat.

This pie is also good served cold with a dollop of whipped cream or non-dairy whipped topping.

*If you don't have vanilla powder, stir 1/8 teaspoon vanilla extract into mix when adding water or substitute vanilla sugar for granulated sugar (vanilla sugar recipe on page 6).

Chocolate Chip Pie Mix

2-1/2 tablespoons brown sugar, firmly packed
2 tablespoons flour
2 tablespoons semi-sweet chocolate chips
1 tablespoon finely chopped pecans
1 teaspoon egg white powder
1/8 teaspoon vanilla powder (optional—see page 6)
1/16 teaspoon baking powder
Dash of salt

Blend all ingredients together and place in a small zipper-type bag if using at a later date or giving as a gift.

To prepare: Microwave 1 tablespoon butter or margarine in mug until melted (about 20 seconds on high power).

Empty pie mix into mug and add 2-1/2 tablespoons water; stirring with a fork until blended.

Microwave on 60% power for 2 minutes. Let stand in the microwave 2 minutes. Remove from oven and let stand until cool enough to eat.

Coconut Cream Pie Mix

2-1/2 tablespoons granulated sugar
2 tablespoons sweetened, flaked coconut, packed
1 tablespoon instant nonfat dry milk
1 tablespoon flour
1-1/2 teaspoons egg white powder
1/8 teaspoon vanilla powder (optional—see page 6)
1/16 teaspoon baking powder
Dash of salt

Blend all ingredients together and place in a small zipper-type bag if using at a later date or giving as a gift.

To prepare: Microwave 1-1/2 tablespoons butter or margarine in mug until melted (about 20 seconds on high power).

Empty pie mix into mug and add 2-1/2 tablespoons of water. Stir with a fork until well blended.

Microwave on 60% power for 2 minutes. Let stand in the microwave 2 minutes. Remove from oven and let stand until cool enough to eat.

This pie is also good served cold with a dollop of whipped cream or non-dairy whipped topping.

Pecan Pie Mix

3 tablespoons finely chopped pecans
3 tablespoons brown sugar, firmly packed
1 tablespoon flour
2 teaspoons egg white powder
1/2 tablespoon instant nonfat dry milk
1/8 teaspoon vanilla powder (optional—see page 6)
1/16 teaspoon baking powder
Dash of salt

Blend all ingredients together and place in a small zipper-type bag if using at a later date or giving as a gift.

To prepare: Microwave 1-1/2 tablespoons butter or margarine in mug until melted (about 20 seconds on high power).

Empty pie mix into mug and add 3 tablespoons of water; stirring with a fork until blended.

Microwave on 60% power for 2 minutes. Let stand in the microwave 2 minutes. Remove from oven and let stand until cool enough to eat.

Sweet Potato Pie Mix

1-1/2 tablespoons granulated sugar
1 tablespoon flour
1 tablespoon instant nonfat dry milk
1 teaspoon egg white powder
1/4 teaspoon ground cinnamon
1/8 teaspoon vanilla powder (optional—see page 6)
1/16 teaspoon baking powder
Dash of salt

Blend all ingredients and place in a small zipper-type bag if using at a later date or giving as a gift.

Additional Ingredients: One (2.5 ounce) jar of pureed sweet potatoes (baby food)

To prepare: Microwave 1/2 tablespoon butter or margarine in mug until melted.

Stir entire jar of sweet potatoes into mug. Add pie mix and 2 tablespoons water; stirring with a fork until blended.

Microwave on 60% power for 2 minutes. Let stand in the microwave 2 minutes. Remove and let stand until cool enough to eat.

Blueberry Cobbler Mix

2 tablespoons flour
2 tablespoons granulated sugar
1 tablespoon instant nonfat dry milk
1 teaspoon egg white powder
1/16 teaspoon baking powder
1/8 teaspoon ground cinnamon
Dash of salt

Blend all ingredients and place in a small zipper-type bag if using at a later date or giving as a gift.

In a separate zipper-type bag, place:
   1/4 cup finely chopped dried blueberries

To prepare: Place blueberries in a mug and add 3 tablespoons of water. Microwave on high power 1 minute or until boiling. Cover and let stand 5 minutes.

Stir in 1/2 tablespoon butter or margarine until melted. Empty cobbler mix into mug. Add 1-1/2 tablespoons water. Stir with a fork until well blended.

Microwave on 60% power for 2 minutes. Let stand in microwave 2 minutes. Remove and let stand until cool enough to eat.

Top with a scoop of ice cream for an extra special treat.

Peach Cobbler Mix

2 tablespoons granulated sugar
2 tablespoons flour
1 tablespoon instant nonfat dry milk
1/8 teaspoon baking powder
1/8 teaspoon cinnamon
Dash of salt

Blend all ingredients and place in a small zipper-type bag if using at a later date or giving as a gift.

Additional ingredients:

1 (4 oz.) snack size container of diced peaches

To prepare: Microwave 1 tablespoon butter or margarine in mug until melted. Add cobbler mix and 2 tablespoons water. Stir with a fork until well blended. Add well-drained peaches on top of batter. Do not stir.

Microwave for 2 minutes on 70% power. Let stand in microwave 2 minutes. Remove from oven and let stand until cool enough to eat.

Peach Crisp Mix

2 tablespoons quick cooking oats (not instant)
1 tablespoon granulated sugar
1 tablespoon brown sugar, firmly packed
1 tablespoon flour
1 tablespoon finely chopped pecans
1/8 teaspoon ground cinnamon
Dash of salt

Blend all ingredients and place in a small zipper-type bag if using at a later date or giving as a gift.

Additional ingredients:
1 (4 oz.) snack size container of diced peaches

To prepare: Microwave 1 tablespoon margarine in mug until melted. Add crisp mix and blend well. Stir in well-drained peaches and microwave 2 minutes on 60% power. Let stand in microwave 2 minutes. Remove from oven and let stand until cool enough to eat.

Pear Crisp Mix

Substitute 1 (4 ounce) snack size container of diced pears for the peaches in the Peach Crisp Mix recipe.

Prepare as directed for Peach Crisp.

Dessert Mixes

Puddings

Chocolate Pudding Mix

(Use an EXTRA LARGE mug for this recipe to help prevent it from boiling over.)

1/4 cup semisweet chocolate chips (mini chips are best)
3 tablespoons instant nonfat dry milk
1 tablespoon granulated sugar
2 teaspoons cornstarch
1/8 teaspoon vanilla powder* (optional)
Dash of salt

Blend ingredients together. Place in a small zipper-type bag if using at a later date or giving as a gift.

To prepare: Empty mix into a LARGE mug (at least 16 ounces) and add 1/2 cup of water.

Stir to blend. Microwave on high power 2 minutes or until boiling and slightly thickened; stirring after each 30 seconds.

Watch carefully, it can boil over! If pudding begins to boil up to top of mug, stop microwave for 10-15 seconds, then resume cooking.

Remove from oven and let stand until cool enough to eat. Serve warm or chilled.

*If you don't have vanilla powder, you can stir 1/8 teaspoon vanilla extract into mix when adding water.

Butterscotch Pudding Mix

(Use an EXTRA LARGE mug for this recipe to help prevent it from boiling over.)

1/4 cup butterscotch baking chips
3 tablespoons instant nonfat dry milk
2 teaspoons brown sugar, firmly packed
2 teaspoons cornstarch
1/8 teaspoon vanilla powder* (optional)
Dash of salt

Blend ingredients together. Place in a small zipper-type bag if using at a later date or giving as a gift.

To prepare: Empty mix into a LARGE mug (at least 16 ounces) and add 1/2 cup of water.

Stir to blend. Microwave on high power 2 minutes or until boiling and slightly thickened; stirring after each 30 seconds.

Watch carefully, it can boil over! If pudding begins to boil up to top of mug, stop microwave for 10-15 seconds, then resume cooking.

Remove from oven and let stand until cool enough to eat. Serve warm or chilled.

Top with whipped cream or non-dairy whipped topping if desired.

*If you don't have vanilla powder, you can stir 1/8 teaspoon vanilla extract into mix when adding water.

Coconut Cream Pudding Mix

(Use an EXTRA LARGE mug for this recipe to help prevent it from boiling over.)

3 tablespoons instant nonfat dry milk
2 tablespoons granulated sugar
2 tablespoons sweetened, flaked coconut, firmly packed
1 tablespoon cornstarch
1/8 teaspoon vanilla powder*
Dash of salt

Blend ingredients together. Place in a small zipper-type bag if using at a later date or giving as a gift.

To prepare: Empty mix into a LARGE mug (at least 16 ounces) and add 1/2 cup of water and 1 teaspoon butter or margarine.

Stir to blend. Microwave on high power 1-1/2 to 2 minutes or until boiling and slightly thickened; stirring after each 30 seconds.

Watch carefully, it can boil over! If pudding begins to boil up to top of mug, stop microwave for 10-15 seconds, then resume cooking.

Remove from oven and let stand until cool enough to eat. Serve warm or chilled.

*If you don't have vanilla powder, stir 1/8 teaspoon vanilla extract into mix when adding water or substitute vanilla sugar for granulated sugar (vanilla sugar recipe on page 6).

Blueberry Bread Pudding Mix

1/4 cup plain, dry bread crumbs
2 tablespoons granulated sugar
2 tablespoons dried blueberries, finely chopped
  (or use dried cherries, peaches or apricots)
1-1/2 tablespoons instant nonfat dry milk
1 teaspoon egg white powder
1/8 teaspoon vanilla powder (optional—see page 6)

Blend ingredients together. Place in a small zipper-type bag if using at a later date or giving as a gift.

Additional ingredients: Cinnamon Sugar
(Make your own cinnamon sugar by mixing 1 tablespoon sugar with 1/4 teaspoon ground cinnamon. Store in an airtight container.)

To prepare pudding: Microwave 1 tablespoon butter or margarine in mug until melted (about 20 seconds on high power). Empty pudding mix into mug and add 1/4 cup water; stirring with a fork until blended. Let batter stand 5 minutes before cooking to partially rehydrate fruit and bread crumbs. Sprinkle 1/2 teaspoon cinnamon sugar over batter.

Microwave on 50% power for 3 minutes. Let stand in microwave for 2 minutes. Remove from oven and let stand until cool enough to eat.

Serve with Vanilla Sauce (recipe on page 62) for an extra-tasty treat!

Chocolate Nut Bread Pudding Mix

1/4 cup plain, dry bread crumbs
2 tablespoons granulated sugar
1-1/2 tablespoons instant nonfat dry milk
1 tablespoon unsweetened cocoa powder
1 tablespoon finely chopped pecans
1 tablespoon semi-sweet chocolate chips
1 teaspoon egg white powder
1/8 teaspoon vanilla powder* (optional)

Blend ingredients together. Place in a small zipper-type bag if using at a later date or giving as a gift.

To prepare pudding: Microwave 1 tablespoon butter or margarine in mug until melted (about 20 seconds on high power). Empty pudding mix into mug and add 1/4 cup water; stirring with a fork until blended.

Let batter stand 5 minutes before cooking to rehydrate bread crumbs. Microwave on 50% power for 3 minutes. Let stand in microwave for 2 minutes. Remove from oven and let stand until cool enough to eat.

Serve with Hot Fudge Sauce (recipe on page 58) for an extra-decadent treat!

*If you don't have vanilla powder, stir 1/8 teaspoon vanilla extract into mix when adding water or substitute vanilla sugar for granulated sugar (vanilla sugar recipe on page 6).

Rice Pudding Mix

2 tablespoons instant nonfat dry milk
2-1/2 tablespoons granulated sugar
1 teaspoon egg white powder
1/8 teaspoon vanilla powder* (optional)
1/8 teaspoon ground cinnamon
1/16 teaspoon ground nutmeg
Dash of salt

Blend all ingredients together. Place in a small zipper-type bag if using at a later date or giving as a gift.

Additional Ingredients:
In a separate zipper-type bag, place 1/3 cup instant rice.

To prepare: Place rice in mug and add 1/4 cup water. Microwave on high power for 1 minute or until boiling. Cover and let stand in microwave 5 minutes.

Remove mug from oven and stir in 1/2 tablespoon butter or margarine until melted. Add 1/4 cup of water and pudding mix. Stir with a fork to blend.

Microwave on 60% power for 2 minutes. *Watch carefully, it can boil over!* Cover and let stand in oven 3 minutes. Remove and let stand (uncovered) until cool enough to eat.

*If you don't have vanilla powder, stir 1/8 teaspoon vanilla extract into mix when adding water or substitute vanilla sugar for granulated sugar (vanilla sugar recipe on page 6).

Apple Rice Pudding Mix

Use the same recipe as the Rice Pudding Mix, but add 1 tablespoon of finely chopped, dried apples (or dried peaches or apricots) to the bag of instant rice.

To prepare: Place the rice and fruit in a mug and add 1/4 cup water. Microwave on high power for 1 minute or until boiling. Cover and let stand in microwave 5 minutes.

Remove mug from oven and stir in 1/2 tablespoon butter or margarine until melted.

Add 1/4 cup water and pudding mix. Stir with a fork to blend.

Microwave on 60% power for 2 minutes. *Watch carefully, it can boil over!* Cover and let stand in oven 3 minutes.

Remove and let stand (uncovered) until cool enough to eat.

Dessert Mixes

Sauces

Hot Fudge Sauce Mix

1-1/2 tablespoons granulated sugar
1/2 tablespoon brown sugar, firmly packed
1/2 tablespoon instant nonfat dry milk
2 teaspoons unsweetened cocoa powder
1 teaspoon cornstarch
1/8 teaspoon vanilla powder (optional—see page 6)

Blend ingredients together and place in a small zipper-type bag if using at a later date or giving as a gift.

To prepare: Microwave 1 teaspoon butter or margarine in mug until melted (about 10 seconds on high power). Empty sauce mix into mug and add 3 tablespoons of water; stirring with a fork to blend.

Microwave on high power 1 to 1-1/2 minutes or until boiling and thickened; stirring after each 30 seconds. *Watch carefully it can boil over!* Remove from microwave and let stand until cool enough to eat.

Serve over ice cream, pound cake or brownies.

Butterscotch Sauce Mix

2 tablespoons brown sugar, firmly packed
1/2 tablespoon instant nonfat dry milk
1 teaspoon cornstarch
1/8 teaspoon vanilla powder* (optional)
Dash of salt (very light)

Blend ingredients and place in a small zipper-type bag if using at a later date or giving as a gift.

To prepare: Microwave 1 teaspoon butter or margarine in mug until melted (about 10 seconds on high power).

Empty sauce mix into mug and add 3 tablespoons of water; stirring with a fork to blend.

Microwave on high power 1 to 1-1/2 minutes or until boiling and thickened; stirring after each 30 seconds. Remove from microwave and let stand until cool enough to eat.

Serve over ice cream or pound cake.

*If you don't have vanilla powder, stir 1/8 teaspoon vanilla extract into sauce when adding water or substitute vanilla-flavored brown sugar for brown sugar in recipe (vanilla sugar recipes on page 6).

Blueberry Sauce Mix

1 tablespoon granulated sugar
1 teaspoon cornstarch
1/8 teaspoon dried, grated lemon peel
1/16 teaspoon vanilla powder (optional—see page 6)

Blend ingredients together and bundle in a double layer of plastic wrap; securing with a twist tie.

Additional Ingredients:
In a separate piece of plastic wrap, bundle 2 tablespoons dried blueberries, finely chopped, and secure with a twist tie.

To prepare: Place blueberries in a mug with 3 tablespoons of water. Microwave on high power about 1 minute or until boiling. Cover and let stand 5 minutes to rehydrate fruit.

Stir in 1 teaspoon butter until melted. Add sauce mix and stir until blended. Microwave on high power about 45 seconds, stirring after each 20-30 seconds until sauce is boiling and thickened. Cover and let stand 5 minutes. Remove cover and let stand until cool enough to eat.

Serve over ice cream or pound cake.

Cherry Sauce Mix

Substitute 2 tablespoons of finely chopped, dried cherries for the dried blueberries in the recipe above. Prepare as directed for Blueberry Sauce.

Peach Sauce Mix

1 tablespoon granulated sugar
1 teaspoon cornstarch
1/8 teaspoon vanilla powder (optional—see page 6)
Pinch of cinnamon (less than 1/6 teaspoon)

Blend ingredients together and bundle in a double layer of plastic wrap; securing with a twist tie.

Additional ingredients:

1 (4 oz.) snack size container of diced peaches

To prepare: Microwave 1 teaspoon of butter or margarine in mug until melted.

Drain peaches, reserving 2 tablespoons of peach juice. Add reserved peach juice to mug. Stir in sauce mix and 3 tablespoons of peaches.

Microwave on high power 1 to 1-1/2 minutes or until sauce is boiling and thickened; stirring after each 30 seconds. Let stand until cool enough to eat.

Serve over ice cream or pound cake.

Vanilla Sauce Mix

2 tablespoons granulated sugar
1/2 tablespoon instant nonfat dry milk
1 teaspoon cornstarch
1/8 teaspoon vanilla powder*

Blend ingredients and place in a small zipper-type bag if using at a later date or giving as a gift.

To prepare: Microwave 1 teaspoon butter or margarine in mug until melted (about 10 seconds on high power).

Empty sauce mix into mug and add 3 tablespoons of water; stirring with a fork to blend.

Microwave on high power 1 to 1-1/2 minutes or until boiling and thickened; stirring after each 30 seconds. Remove from microwave and let stand until cool enough to eat.

Drizzle over Blueberry Bread Pudding (recipe on page 53) or pound cake.

*If you don't have vanilla powder, stir 1/8 teaspoon vanilla extract into sauce when adding water or substitute vanilla sugar for granulated sugar in recipe (vanilla sugar recipe on page 6).

Lemon Sauce Mix

1 tablespoon granulated sugar
2 teaspoons presweetened lemonade mix
1 teaspoon cornstarch

Blend ingredients and place in a small zipper-type bag if using at a later date or giving as a gift.

To prepare: Microwave 1 teaspoon butter or margarine in mug until melted (about 10 seconds on high power).

Empty sauce mix into mug and add 2-1/2 tablespoons of water; stirring with a fork to blend.

Microwave on high power 1 to 1-1/2 minutes or until boiling and thickened; stirring after each 30 seconds. Remove from microwave and let stand until cool enough to eat.

Drizzle over Blueberry Bread Pudding (recipe on page 53) or pound cake

Praline Sauce Mix

2 tablespoons brown sugar, firmly packed
1 tablespoon pecans, finely chopped
1/2 tablespoon instant nonfat dry milk
1 teaspoon cornstarch
1/8 teaspoon vanilla powder* (optional)
Dash of salt (very light)

Blend ingredients and place in a small zipper-type bag if using at a later date or giving as a gift.

To prepare: Microwave 1 teaspoon butter or margarine in mug until melted (about 10 seconds on high power). Empty sauce mix into mug and add 3 tablespoons of water; stirring with a fork to blend.

Microwave on high power 1 to 1-1/2 minutes or until boiling and thickened; stirring after each 30 seconds. Remove from microwave and let stand until cool enough to eat.

Serve over ice cream or pound cake.

*If you don't have vanilla powder, stir 1/8 teaspoon vanilla extract into sauce when adding water or substitute vanilla-flavored brown sugar for brown sugar in the recipe (vanilla sugar recipes on page 6).

Breakfast Treat Mixes

Coffee Cakes

Blueberry Lemon Coffee Cake

1/4 cup flour
3 tablespoons granulated sugar
1 tablespoon instant nonfat dry milk
1 tablespoon dried blueberries, finely chopped
1 teaspoon egg white powder
1/4 teaspoon baking powder
1/4 teaspoon dried grated lemon peel
Dash of salt

Blend ingredients and place in a small zipper-type bag if using at a later date or giving as a gift.

Lemon Glaze Mix
In a separate small zipper-type bag, combine the following ingredients:
> 1/3 cup powdered sugar
> 1 teaspoon presweetened lemonade mix

To prepare cake: Microwave 1-1/2 tablespoons butter or margarine in mug until melted (about 20 seconds on high power). Empty cake mix into mug and add 3 tablespoons water; stirring with a fork until blended. (Optional: Let batter stand 5 minutes before cooking to partially rehydrate fruit if desired.) Microwave on 60% power for 2 minutes. Let stand in oven 2 minutes. Cool slightly before adding glaze.

To make glaze: Add 1-1/2 teaspoons water to glaze mix in zipper-type bag. Close and rub bag until glaze is smooth. Cut off one bottom corner of glaze mix bag and apply glaze to warm cake. -OR- Mix glaze in a small bowl and pour over top of cake. Let cake stand until cool enough to eat.

Cinnamon Crunch Coffee Cake Mix

1/4 cup flour
3 tablespoons granulated sugar
1 tablespoon instant nonfat dry milk
1 teaspoon egg white powder
1/4 teaspoon baking powder
1/4 teaspoon of ground cinnamon
Dash of salt

Blend ingredients together and place in a small zipper-type bag if using at a later date or giving as a gift.

Cinnamon Crunch Topping Mix

Blend together the following and place in another small zipper-type bag or plastic wrap:

> 2 teaspoons brown sugar, packed
> 1 teaspoon finely chopped pecans
> 1/8 teaspoon ground cinnamon

To prepare: Microwave 1-1/2 tablespoons butter or margarine in mug until melted (about 20 seconds on high power).

Empty cake mix into mug and add 3 tablespoons water; stirring with a fork until blended. Sprinkle topping on top of cake batter.

Microwave on 60% power for 2 minutes. Let stand in microwave 2 minutes. Remove from oven and let cake stand until cool enough to eat.

Orange Fudge Coffee Cake Mix

3 tablespoons flour
3 tablespoons granulated sugar
1 tablespoon unsweetened cocoa powder
1 tablespoon instant nonfat dry milk
1 tablespoon semi-sweet chocolate chips (mini chips are best)
1 teaspoon egg white powder
1/4 teaspoon baking powder
1/4 teaspoon dried grated orange peel
1/8 teaspoon ground cinnamon
Dash of salt

Blend ingredients together and place in a zipper-type bag if using at a later date or giving as a gift.

Chocolate Glaze Mix
In a separate small zipper-type bag, combine the following ingredients:

> 1/3 cup powdered sugar
> 1-1/2 teaspoons unsweetened cocoa powder
> 1/2 teaspoon presweetened orange drink mix

To prepare cake: Microwave 1-1/2 tablespoons butter or margarine in mug until melted (about 20 seconds on high power). Empty cake mix into mug and add 3 tablespoons water; stirring with a fork until blended. Microwave on 60% power for 2 minutes. Let stand in microwave 2 minutes. Cool slightly before adding glaze.

To make glaze: Add 1-1/2 teaspoons water to glaze mix in zipper-type bag. Close and rub bag until glaze is smooth. Cut off one bottom corner of glaze mix bag and apply glaze to warm cake. -OR- Mix glaze in a small bowl and pour on top of cake. Let cake stand until cool enough to eat.

Pear Coffee Cake Mix

1/4 cup flour
2-1/2 tablespoons granulated sugar
1 tablespoon instant nonfat dry milk
1 teaspoon egg white powder
1/4 teaspoon baking powder
1/8 teaspoon ground cinnamon
1/8 teaspoon vanilla powder (optional—see page 6)
Dash of salt

Blend ingredients and place in a small zipper-type bag if using at a later date or giving as a gift.

Topping mix:
Blend together the following and wrap in plastic wrap:
>   2 teaspoons brown sugar, packed
>   1 teaspoon finely chopped pecans
>   1/8 teaspoon ground cinnamon

Additional ingredients:
1 (4 ounce) snack size container of diced pears

To prepare: Microwave 1-1/2 tablespoons butter or margarine in mug until melted (about 20 seconds on high power). Empty cake mix into mug and add 3 tablespoons water; stirring with a fork until blended.

Drain juice from pears. Stir two tablespoons of pears into batter. Discard remaining pears or save for another use. Sprinkle batter with topping mix. Microwave on 60% power for 2-1/2 minutes. Let stand in oven 2 minutes. Remove and let stand until cool enough to eat.

Piña Colada Coffee Cake Mix

1/4 cup flour
2 tablespoons granulated sugar
1 tablespoon instant nonfat dry milk
1 tablespoon sweetened, flaked coconut
1 tablespoon finely chopped macadamia nuts (or almonds)
1 teaspoon egg white powder
1/4 teaspoon baking powder
Dash of salt

Blend ingredients and place in a small zipper-type bag if using at a later date or giving as a gift.

Pineapple Glaze Mix
In a separate small zipper-type bag, combine the following ingredients: 1/3 cup powdered sugar

Additional ingredients:
1 (4 ounce) snack size container of pineapple tidbits

To prepare cake: Microwave 1-1/2 tablespoons butter or margarine in mug until melted (about 20 seconds on high power). Empty cake mix into mug and add 3 tablespoons water; stirring with a fork until blended. Drain juice from pineapple, reserving 1-1/2 teaspoons for glaze. Stir two tablespoons of tidbits into batter. (Smash the tidbits with a fork before adding to batter if desired.) Microwave on 60% power for 2-1/2 minutes. Let stand in oven 2 minutes. Cool slightly before adding glaze.

To make glaze: Add 1-1/2 teaspoons reserved pineapple juice to glaze mix in zipper-type bag. Close and rub bag until glaze is smooth. Cut off one bottom corner of glaze mix bag and apply glaze to warm cake. –OR- Mix glaze in a small bowl and pour on top of warm cake. Let cake stand until cool enough to eat.

Mango Coffee Cake Mix

1/4 cup flour
2-1/2 tablespoons sugar
1 tablespoon instant nonfat dry milk
1 teaspoon egg white powder
1/4 teaspoon baking powder
1/8 teaspoon ground cinnamon
1/8 teaspoon vanilla powder* (optional)
Dash of salt

Blend ingredients and place in a small zipper-type bag if using at a later date or giving as a gift.

Additional ingredients:
1 (2.5 ounce) jar of pureed mangoes (baby food)

Topping Mix:
Blend together the following and wrap in plastic wrap:
 2 teaspoons brown sugar, packed
 2 teaspoons finely chopped pecans
 1/8 teaspoon ground cinnamon

To Prepare: Microwave 1 tablespoon butter or margarine in mug until melted (about 20 seconds on high power). Stir 2 tablespoons of mangoes into mug. Empty cake mix into mug and add 1-1/2 tablespoons water; stirring with a fork until blended. Sprinkle topping mix on top of batter. Microwave on 60% power for 2-1/2 minutes. Let stand in oven 2 minutes. Remove from oven and let stand until cool enough to eat.

*If you don't have vanilla powder, stir 1/8 teaspoon vanilla extract into mix when adding water or substitute vanilla sugar for granulated sugar in recipe (vanilla sugar recipe on page 6).

Mocha Coffee Cake Mix

3 tablespoons flour
3 tablespoons granulated sugar
1 tablespoon unsweetened cocoa
1 tablespoon instant nonfat dry milk
2 tablespoons semi-sweet chocolate chips (mini chips are best)
1 teaspoon egg white powder
1/4 teaspoon baking powder
1/4 teaspoon instant coffee granules
1/8 teaspoon vanilla powder (optional—see page 6)
Dash of salt

Blend ingredients together and place in a small zipper-type bag if using at a later date or giving as a gift.

Chocolate Glaze Mix
In a separate small zipper-type bag, combine the following ingredients:

>   1/3 cup powdered sugar
>   1-1/2 teaspoons unsweetened cocoa powder

To prepare cake: Microwave 1-1/2 tablespoons butter or margarine in mug until melted. Empty cake mix into mug and add 3 tablespoons water; stirring with a fork until blended and coffee granules are melted. Microwave on 60% power for 2 minutes. Let stand in oven 2 minutes. Let cool slightly before adding glaze.

To make glaze: Add 1-1/2 teaspoons water (or coffee) to glaze mix in zipper-type bag. Close and rub bag until glaze is smooth. Cut off one bottom corner of glaze mix bag and apply glaze to warm cake. –OR- Mix glaze in a small bowl and pour on top of cake. Let cake stand until cool enough to eat.

Breakfast Treat Mixes

Fruit Breads

Amaretto Peach Bread Mix

1/4 cup flour
3 tablespoons granulated sugar
1 tablespoon instant nonfat dry milk
1 tablespoon finely chopped almonds
1 teaspoon egg white powder
1 teaspoon Amaretto flavored powdered coffee creamer
1/4 teaspoon baking powder
Dash of salt

Blend ingredients and place in a small zipper-type bag if using at a later date or giving as a gift.

Amaretto Glaze Mix
In a separate small zipper-type bag, combine the following ingredients:
 1/3 cup powdered sugar
 1 teaspoon Amaretto flavored powdered coffee creamer

Additional ingredients:
1 (4 ounce) snack size container of diced peaches

To prepare: Microwave 1-1/2 tablespoons butter or margarine in mug until melted. Empty bread mix into mug and add 3 tablespoons water; stirring with a fork until blended. Drain juice from peaches, reserving 1-1/2 teaspoons for glaze. Stir two tablespoons of well-drained peaches into batter. Microwave on 60% power for 2-1/2 minutes. Let stand in oven 2 minutes. Let cool slightly before adding glaze.

To make glaze: Add 1-1/2 teaspoons reserved peach juice to glaze mix in zipper-type bag. Close and rub bag until glaze is smooth. Cut off one bottom corner of glaze mix bag and apply glaze to warm bread. -OR- Mix glaze in a small bowl and pour over top of warm bread. Let bread stand until cool enough to eat.

Apple Nut Bread Mix

1/4 cup flour
3 tablespoons brown sugar, packed
1 tablespoon finely chopped pecans
1 teaspoon egg white powder
1/4 teaspoon ground cinnamon
1/4 teaspoon baking powder
1/8 teaspoon vanilla powder (optional—see page 6)
Dash of salt

Blend ingredients and place in a small zipper-type bag if using at a later date or giving as a gift.

In a separate zipper-type bag place:
2 tablespoons finely chopped dried apples

Additional ingredients:
Cinnamon Sugar* (optional)

To prepare: Place apples in mug and add 2 tablespoons of water. Microwave on high power about 45 seconds or until boiling. Cover and let stand in the microwave for 5 minutes. Remove from oven and stir in 1-1/2 tablespoons butter or margarine until melted. Empty mix into mug and add 2 tablespoons of water. Stir with a fork until well blended. Sprinkle about 1/2 teaspoon of Cinnamon Sugar on top of batter. Microwave on 60% power for 2 minutes. Let stand in the oven 2 minutes. Remove from oven and let stand until cool enough to eat.

*Make your own cinnamon sugar by mixing 1 tablespoon granulated sugar with 1/4 teaspoon ground cinnamon. Store in an airtight container.

Banana Nut Bread Mix

1/4 cup flour
3 tablespoons granulated sugar
1 tablespoon finely chopped pecans
1 teaspoon egg white powder
1/4 teaspoon ground cinnamon
1/4 teaspoon baking powder
1/8 teaspoon vanilla powder (optional—see page 6)
Dash of salt

Blend ingredients together and place in a small zipper-type bag if using at a later date or giving as a gift.

Additional ingredients:

1 (2.5 ounce) jar of pureed bananas (baby food)
Cinnamon Sugar (optional)*

To prepare: Microwave 1 tablespoon butter or margarine in mug until melted (about 20 seconds on high power). Stir 2 tablespoons of bananas into mug. Empty bread mix into mug and add 1-1/2 tablespoons water; stirring with a fork until blended.

Optional: Sprinkle about 1/2 teaspoon of Cinnamon Sugar on top of batter. Microwave on 60% power for 2-1/2 minutes. Let stand in oven 2 minutes. Remove from oven and let stand until cool enough to eat.

*Make your own cinnamon sugar by mixing 1 tablespoon granulated sugar with 1/4 teaspoon ground cinnamon. Store in an airtight container.

Cherry Pecan Bread Mix

1/4 cup flour
2 tablespoons granulated sugar
2 tablespoons finely chopped dried cherries
1 tablespoon finely chopped pecans
1 tablespoon instant nonfat dry milk
1 teaspoon egg white powder
1/4 teaspoon baking powder
1/8 teaspoon vanilla powder (optional—see page 6)
Dash of salt

Blend ingredients and place in a small zipper-type bag if using at a later date or giving as a gift.

Glaze Mix
In a separate small zipper-type bag combine the following ingredients:
      1/3 cup powdered sugar
      1/8 teaspoon vanilla powder (optional)

To prepare bread: Microwave 1-1/2 tablespoons butter or margarine in mug until melted. Empty bread mix into mug and add 3 tablespoons water; stirring with a fork until blended. (Optional: Let batter stand 5 minutes before cooking to partially rehydrate fruit if desired.) Microwave on 60% power for 2 minutes. Let stand in microwave for 2 minutes. Cool slightly before adding glaze.

To make glaze: Add 1-1/2 teaspoons water to glaze mix in zipper-type bag. Close and gently rub bag until glaze is smooth. Cut off one bottom corner of glaze mix bag and apply glaze to warm bread. -OR- Mix glaze in a small bowl and pour over top of bread. Let stand until cool enough to eat.

Cranberry Orange Bread Mix

1/4 cup flour
3 tablespoons granulated sugar
1 tablespoon instant nonfat dry milk
2 tablespoons dried cranberries, finely chopped
1 teaspoon egg white powder
1/4 teaspoon baking powder
1/4 teaspoon dried grated orange peel
Dash of salt

Blend ingredients and place in a small zipper-type bag if using at a later date or giving as a gift.

Orange Glaze Mix
In a separate small zipper-type bag, combine the following ingredients:

> 1/3 cup powdered sugar
> 1 teaspoon presweetened orange drink mix

To prepare cake: Microwave 1-1/2 tablespoons butter or margarine in mug until melted. Empty bread mix into mug and add 3 tablespoons water; stirring with a fork until blended. (Optional: Let batter stand 5 minutes before cooking to partially rehydrate fruit if desired.) Microwave on 60% power for 2 minutes. Let stand in oven 2 minutes. Let cool slightly before adding glaze.

To make glaze: Add 1-1/2 teaspoons water to glaze mix in zipper-type bag. Close and rub bag until glaze is smooth. Cut off one bottom corner of glaze mix bag and apply glaze to warm bread. -OR- Mix glaze in a small bowl and pour over top of bread. Let cake stand until cool enough to eat.

Breakfast Treat Mixes

Muffins

Applesauce Oatmeal Muffin Mix

3 tablespoons brown sugar, packed
2-1/2 tablespoons flour
1-1/2 tablespoons quick cooking oats
1 teaspoon egg white powder
1/4 teaspoon ground cinnamon
1/8 teaspoon baking soda
1/8 teaspoon vanilla powder (optional—see page 6)
1/16 teaspoon ground nutmeg
Pinch of ground cloves (less than 1/16 teaspoon)
Dash of salt

Blend ingredients together and place in a small zipper-type bag if using at a later date or giving as a gift.

Additional ingredients:
1 (2.5 ounce) jar of applesauce (baby food)

Cinnamon Sugar (optional)
(Make your own cinnamon sugar by mixing 1 tablespoon granulated sugar with 1/4 teaspoon ground cinnamon. Store in an airtight container.)

To prepare: Microwave 1 tablespoon butter or margarine in mug until melted (about 20 seconds on high power). Stir 2 tablespoons of applesauce into mug. Empty mix into mug and add 1-1/2 tablespoons water; stirring with a fork until blended.

Optional: Sprinkle about 1/2 teaspoon of Cinnamon Sugar on top of batter. Microwave on 60% power for 2-1/2 minutes. Let stand in oven 2 minutes. Remove from oven and let stand until cool enough to eat.

Blueberry White Chocolate Muffin Mix

1/4 cup flour
3 tablespoons granulated sugar
1-1/2 tablespoons finely chopped dried blueberries
1 tablespoon white chocolate chips (optional)
1 tablespoon instant nonfat dry milk
1 teaspoon egg white powder
1/4 teaspoon baking powder
1/8 teaspoon vanilla powder (optional—see page 6)
Dash of salt

Blend ingredients and place in a small zipper-type bag.

Additional ingredients: Cinnamon Sugar
(Make your own cinnamon sugar by mixing 1 tablespoon granulated sugar with 1/4 teaspoon ground cinnamon. Store in a small airtight container.)

To prepare: Microwave 1-1/2 tablespoons butter or margarine in mug until melted. Empty muffin mix into mug and add 3 tablespoons water; stirring with a fork until blended.

(Optional: Let batter stand 5 minutes before cooking to partially rehydrate fruit if desired.) Sprinkle batter with 1/2 teaspoon Cinnamon Sugar.

Microwave on 60% power for 2 minutes. Let stand in oven 2 minutes. Remove and let stand until cool enough to eat.

Cappuccino Chocolate Chip Muffin Mix

1/4 cup flour
3 tablespoons granulated sugar
2 tablespoons semi-sweet chocolate chips (mini chips are best)
1 tablespoon instant nonfat dry milk
1 teaspoon egg white powder
1/4 teaspoon baking powder
1/4 teaspoon ground cinnamon
1/4 teaspoon instant coffee granules
Dash of salt

Blend ingredients together and place in a small zipper-type bag if using at a later date or giving as a gift.

Additional Ingredients:
Cinnamon Sugar (optional)*

To prepare: Microwave 1-1/2 tablespoons butter or margarine in mug until melted. Empty mix into mug and add 3 tablespoons water; stirring with a fork until blended and coffee granules are melted.

Sprinkle the top of the batter with 1/2 teaspoon of Cinnamon Sugar before baking, if desired.

Microwave on 60% power for 2 minutes. Let stand in microwave 2 minutes. Remove from oven and let stand until cool enough to eat.

*Make your own cinnamon sugar by mixing 1 tablespoon granulated sugar with 1/4 teaspoon ground cinnamon. Store in a small airtight container.

Pineapple Muffin Mix

1/4 cup flour
2 tablespoons granulated sugar
1 tablespoon instant nonfat dry milk
1 teaspoon egg white powder
1/4 teaspoon baking powder
1/8 teaspoon vanilla powder (optional—see page 6)
Dash of salt

Blend ingredients together and place in a small zipper-type bag if using at a later date or giving as a gift.

Topping mix:
In a separate small zipper-type bag or plastic wrap, combine the following ingredients:

> 2 teaspoons brown sugar, packed
> 1/8 teaspoon ground cinnamon

Additional ingredients:
1 (4 ounce) snack size container of pineapple tidbits

To prepare: Microwave 1-1/2 tablespoons butter or margarine in mug until melted. Empty muffin mix into mug and add 3 tablespoons water; stirring with a fork until blended.

Drain juice from pineapple. Stir two tablespoons of tidbits into batter. (Smash the tidbits with a fork before adding to batter if desired.) Discard remaining pineapple or save for another use.

Sprinkle batter with topping mix. Microwave on 60% power for 2-1/2 minutes. Let stand in oven 2 minutes. Remove from oven and let stand until cool enough to eat.

Sweet Potato Muffin Mix

1/4 cup flour
3 tablespoons granulated sugar
1 tablespoon finely chopped pecans
1 teaspoon egg white powder
1/4 teaspoon ground cinnamon
1/4 teaspoon baking powder
1/8 teaspoon vanilla powder (optional—see page 6)
Dash of salt

Blend ingredients together and place in a small zipper-type bag if using at a later date or giving as a gift.

Additional ingredients:
1 (2.5 ounce) jar of pureed sweet potatoes (baby food)
Cinnamon Sugar (optional)*

To prepare: Microwave 1 tablespoon butter or margarine in mug until melted (about 20 seconds on high power).

Stir 2 tablespoons of sweet potatoes into mug. Empty muffin mix into mug and add 1-1/2 tablespoons water; stirring with a fork until blended.

Optional: Sprinkle about 1/2 teaspoon of Cinnamon Sugar on top of batter. Microwave on 60% power for 2-1/2 minutes. Let stand in oven 2 minutes. Remove from oven and let stand until cool enough to eat.

*Make your own cinnamon sugar by mixing 1 tablespoon granulated sugar with 1/4 teaspoon ground cinnamon. Store in a small airtight container.

Breakfast Treat Mixes

Scones

Coffee Banana Scone Mix

1/4 cup flour
3 tablespoons granulated sugar
1 tablespoon finely chopped walnuts
1 tablespoon instant nonfat milk
1 teaspoon egg white powder
1/4 teaspoon baking powder
1/4 teaspoon instant coffee granules
1/8 teaspoon vanilla powder (optional—see page 6)
Dash of salt

Blend ingredients and place in a small zipper-type bag if using at a later date or giving as a gift.

Additional ingredients:
> 1 (2.5 ounce) jar of pureed bananas (baby food)
> Cinnamon Sugar*

To prepare: Microwave 1 tablespoon butter or margarine in mug until melted (about 20 seconds on high power).

Stir in 2 tablespoons of bananas. Empty scone mix into mug and add 1-1/2 tablespoons water; stirring with a fork until blended.

Sprinkle about 1/2 teaspoon of Cinnamon Sugar on top of batter. Microwave on 60% power for 2-1/2 minutes. Let stand in oven 2 minutes. Remove from oven and let stand until cool enough to eat.

*Make your own cinnamon sugar by mixing 1 tablespoon granulated sugar with 1/4 teaspoon ground cinnamon. Store in an airtight container.

Cranberry Oat Scone Mix

3 tablespoons flour
1-1/2 tablespoons quick-cooking oats
2-1/2 tablespoons granulated sugar
1 tablespoon instant nonfat dry milk
1 teaspoon egg white powder
1/4 teaspoon baking powder
Dash of salt
2 tablespoons dried cranberries, finely chopped

Blend ingredients together and place in a small zipper-type bag if using at a later date or giving as a gift.

Topping Mix:
Blend together the following and bundle in a piece of plastic wrap:

> 2 teaspoons brown sugar, packed
> 1/8 teaspoon cinnamon

To prepare: Microwave 1-1/2 tablespoons butter or margarine in mug until melted (about 20 seconds on high power).

Empty scone mix into mug. Add 3 tablespoons water and stir with a fork until blended. (Optional: Let batter stand 5 minutes before cooking to partially rehydrate fruit if desired.)

Sprinkle topping mix on top of batter and microwave on 60% power for 2 minutes. Let stand in microwave for 2 minutes. Remove from microwave and let stand until cool enough to eat.

Gingerbread Raisin Scone Mix

1/4 cup flour
3 tablespoons brown sugar, firmly packed
2 tablespoons raisins
1 tablespoon instant nonfat dry milk
1 teaspoon egg white powder
1/4 teaspoon baking powder
1/8 teaspoon ground cinnamon
1/16 teaspoon ground ginger
Pinch of ground cloves (less than 1/16 teaspoon)
Dash of salt

Blend ingredients together and place in a small zipper-type bag if using at a later date or giving as a gift.

Additional ingredients:
Cinnamon Sugar*

To prepare: Microwave 1-1/2 tablespoons butter or margarine in mug until melted (about 20 seconds on high power).

Empty scone mix into mug. Add 3 tablespoons water and stir with a fork until blended.

Sprinkle 1/2 teaspoon Cinnamon Sugar on top of batter and microwave on 60% power for 2 minutes. Let stand in microwave for 2 minutes. Remove from microwave and let stand until cool enough to eat.

*Make your own cinnamon sugar by mixing 1 tablespoon granulated sugar with 1/4 teaspoon ground cinnamon. Store in an airtight container.

Lemon Walnut Scone Mix

1/4 cup flour
3 tablespoons granulated sugar
1 tablespoon finely chopped walnuts
1 tablespoon instant nonfat milk
1 teaspoon egg white powder
1/4 teaspoon baking powder
1/4 teaspoon dried grated lemon peel
Dash of salt

Blend ingredients and place in a small zipper-type bag if using at a later date or giving as a gift.

Lemon Glaze Mix
In a separate small zipper-type bag, combine the following ingredients:
> 1/3 cup powdered sugar
> 1 teaspoon presweetened lemonade mix

To prepare scone: Microwave 1-1/2 tablespoons butter or margarine in mug until melted (about 20 seconds on high power). Empty scone mix into mug and add 3 tablespoons water; stirring with a fork until blended. Microwave on 60% power for 2 minutes. Let stand in the microwave 2 minutes. Cool slightly before adding glaze.

To make glaze: Add 1-1/2 teaspoons water to glaze mix in zipper-type bag. Close and rub bag until glaze is smooth. Cut off one bottom corner of glaze mix bag and apply glaze to warm scone. -OR- Mix glaze in a small bowl and pour over top of warm scone. Let stand until cool enough to eat.

Peach Scone Mix

1/4 cup flour
3 tablespoons granulated sugar
2 tablespoons finely chopped dried peaches
1 tablespoon instant nonfat dry milk
1 teaspoon egg white powder
1/4 teaspoon baking powder
1/8 teaspoon ground cinnamon
1/16 teaspoon ground nutmeg
Dash of salt

Blend ingredients and place in a small zipper-type bag if using at a later date or giving as a gift.

Additional ingredients:
Cinnamon Sugar (Make your own cinnamon sugar by mixing 1 tablespoon granulated sugar with 1/4 teaspoon ground cinnamon. Store in an airtight container.)

To prepare: Microwave 1-1/2 tablespoons butter or margarine in mug until melted (about 20 seconds on high power).

Empty scone mix into mug. Add 3 tablespoons water and stir with a fork until blended. (Optional: Let batter stand 5 minutes before cooking to partially rehydrate fruit if desired.)

Sprinkle 1/2 teaspoon Cinnamon Sugar on top of batter and microwave on 60% power for 2 minutes. Let stand in microwave 2 minutes. Remove from microwave and let stand until cool enough to eat.

Christmas Scone Mix

1/4 cup flour
1-1/2 tablespoons brown sugar, firmly packed
1-1/2 tablespoons granulated sugar
1-1/2 tablespoons dried cranberries, finely chopped
1 tablespoon chopped pecans
1 tablespoon instant nonfat dry milk
1 teaspoon egg white powder
1/4 teaspoon baking powder
1/4 teaspoon dried grated orange peel (optional)
1/8 teaspoon ground cinnamon
Dash of salt

Blend ingredients together and place in a small zipper-type bag if using at a later date or giving as a gift.

Additional ingredients:
Cinnamon Sugar*

To prepare: Microwave 1-1/2 tablespoons butter or margarine in mug until melted (about 20 seconds on high power).

Empty scone mix into mug. Add 3 tablespoons water and stir with a fork until blended.

Sprinkle 1/2 teaspoon Cinnamon Sugar on top of batter and microwave on 60% power for 2 minutes. Let stand in microwave for 2 minutes. Remove from microwave and let stand until cool enough to eat.

*Make your own cinnamon sugar by mixing 1 tablespoon granulated sugar with 1/4 teaspoon ground cinnamon. Store in an airtight container.

Chocolate Chunk Scone Mix

1/4 cup flour
3 tablespoons granulated sugar
2 tablespoons semi-sweet chocolate chips (mini chips are best)
1 tablespoon instant nonfat dry milk
1 teaspoon egg white powder
1/4 teaspoon baking powder
1/8 teaspoon vanilla powder (optional—see page 6)
Dash of salt

Blend ingredients together and place in a small zipper-type bag if using at a later date or giving as a gift.

Chocolate Glaze Mix

In a separate small zipper-type bag, combine the following ingredients:

> 1/3 cup powdered sugar
> 1-1/2 teaspoons unsweetened cocoa powder

To prepare scone: Microwave 1-1/2 tablespoons butter or margarine in mug until melted. Empty scone mix into mug and add 3 tablespoons water; stirring with a fork until blended.

Microwave on 60% power for 2 minutes. Let stand in microwave 2 minutes. Remove from oven. Cool slightly before adding glaze.

To make glaze: Add 1-1/2 teaspoons water to glaze mix in zipper-type bag. Close and rub bag until glaze is smooth. Cut off one bottom corner of glaze mix bag and apply glaze to warm cake. –OR- Mix glaze in a small bowl and pour on top of cake. Let cake stand until cool enough to eat.

Hot Beverage Mixes

Tea, Cocoa & Coffee

Chai Tea Latte Mix

1/4 cup granulated sugar
2 tablespoons instant nonfat dry milk
2 tablespoons powdered coffee creamer
2 tablespoons powdered French vanilla coffee creamer
2 tablespoons unsweetened instant tea
1/4 teaspoon ground cinnamon
1/4 teaspoon ground ginger
1/16 teaspoon ground cloves

Blend all ingredients and process in blender or food processor until mixture is a fine powder. Place in a small zipper-type bag. Recipe makes 4 servings.

To prepare: Microwave 1 cup of water on high power for 1 to 1-1/2 minutes or until hot. Stir in 3 tablespoons of mix.

Chocolate Tea Mix

1/4 cup brown sugar, firmly packed
3 tablespoons instant nonfat dry milk
2 tablespoons powdered French vanilla coffee creamer
2 tablespoons unsweetened instant tea
1 tablespoon unsweetened cocoa powder

Blend all ingredients and place in a small zipper-type bag. Recipe makes about 4 servings.

To prepare: Microwave 1 cup of water (or 3/4 cup for stronger tea) on high power for 1 to 1-1/2 minutes or until hot. Stir in about 3 tablespoons of mix.

Hot Mulled Tea Mix

3 tablespoons presweetened orange drink mix
3 tablespoons granulated sugar
2 tablespoons unsweetened instant tea
1 tablespoon presweetened lemonade mix
1/4 teaspoon ground cinnamon
1/8 teaspoon ground cloves

Blend all ingredients together. Place in a small zipper-type bag.
Recipe makes about 6 servings.

To prepare: Microwave 1 cup of water on high power for 1 to
1-1/2 minutes or until hot. Stir in about 1-1/2 tablespoons of
mix.

Friendship Tea Mix

1/4 cup presweetened orange drink mix
2 tablespoons granulated sugar
2 tablespoons unsweetened instant tea
1 tablespoon presweetened lemonade mix
1/4 teaspoon ground cinnamon
1/4 teaspoon unsweetened cherry-flavored soft-drink mix
1/8 teaspoon ground nutmeg

Blend all ingredients together. Place in a small zipper-type bag.
Recipe makes about 4-5 servings.

To prepare: Microwave 1 cup of water on high power for 1 to
1-1/2 minutes or until hot. Stir in 1-1/2 to 2 tablespoons of mix.

Mexican Hot Chocolate Mix

1/2 cup instant nonfat dry milk
3 tablespoons brown sugar, firmly packed
2 tablespoons powdered French vanilla coffee creamer
1-1/2 tablespoons unsweetened cocoa powder
1/4 teaspoon ground cinnamon
Dash of salt

Blend all ingredients and place in a small zipper-type bag. Recipe makes about 4 servings.

To prepare: Microwave 3/4 cup of water on high power for 1 to 1-1/2 minutes or until hot. Stir in 3 tablespoons of mix.

If you plan to give this mix as a gift, attach a cinnamon stick to the mug handle with raffia.

Orange Spice Hot Chocolate Mix

1 cup instant nonfat dry milk
2/3 cup semi-sweet chocolate chips
1 tablespoon granulated sugar
1 teaspoon dried grated orange peel
1/2 teaspoon ground cinnamon

Place all ingredients in a food processor or blender and process until finely ground. Transfer to a small zipper-type bag. Recipe makes about 4 - 5 servings.

To prepare: Microwave 3/4 cup of water on high power for 1 to 1-1/2 minutes or until boiling. Stir in about 1/3 cup of mix.

Hot Malted Cocoa Mix

1/4 cup nonfat dry milk powder
1/4 cup granulated sugar
1/4 cup malted milk powder
2 tablespoons powdered coffee creamer
2 tablespoons unsweetened cocoa powder
Dash salt

Blend all ingredients and place in a small zipper-type bag. Recipe makes about 4 servings.

To prepare: Microwave 3/4 cup of water on high power for 1 to 1-1/2 minutes or until hot. Stir in 1/4 cup of mix.

Amaretto Hot Cocoa Mix

1/2 cup instant nonfat dry milk
3 tablespoons granulated sugar
2 tablespoons unsweetened cocoa powder
1-1/2 tablespoons powdered Amaretto flavored coffee creamer
1 tablespoon powdered coffee creamer
Dash of salt

Blend all ingredients and place in a small zipper-type bag. Recipe makes about 4 servings.

To prepare: Microwave 3/4 cup of water on high power for 1 to 1-1/2 minutes or until hot. Stir in 3 to 3-1/2 tablespoons of mix.

Snowman Soup Mix

1 cup instant nonfat dry milk
2/3 cup white chocolate baking chips
3 tablespoons vanilla flavor powdered coffee creamer

Combine all ingredients in a food processor or blender and process until finely ground. Place mix in a small zipper-type bag.

Recipe makes about 1-1/2 cups mix (about 4 servings).

To prepare: Microwave 1 cup of water on high power for 1 to 1-1/2 minutes or until hot. Stir in about 1/3 cup of mix.

Mocha Cappuccino Coffee Mix

3 tablespoons granulated sugar
2 tablespoons powdered coffee creamer
1 tablespoon unsweetened cocoa powder
2 teaspoons instant coffee granules
1/4 teaspoon ground cinnamon

Blend ingredients and place in a small zipper-type bag. Recipe makes about 3 servings.

To prepare: Microwave 3/4 cup of water on high power for 1 to 1-1/2 minutes or until hot. Stir in 2 tablespoons of mix.

Caramel Coffee Mix

1/4 cup powdered coffee creamer
1/4 cup brown sugar, firmly packed
2 tablespoons instant coffee granules

Blend all ingredients and place in a small zipper-type bag. Recipe makes about 5 servings.

To prepare: Microwave 3/4 cup of water on high power for 1 to 1-1/2 minutes or until hot. Stir in 2 tablespoons of mix.

Gingerbread Coffee Mix

1/4 cup powdered coffee creamer
3 tablespoons brown sugar, firmly packed
1 tablespoon instant coffee granules
1/4 teaspoon ground cinnamon
1/8 teaspoon ground ginger
1/8 teaspoon ground nutmeg
1/8 teaspoon ground cloves

Blend all ingredients and place in a small zipper-type bag. Recipe makes about 4 servings.

To prepare: Microwave 3/4 cup of water on high power for 1 to 1-1/2 minutes or until hot. Stir in 2 tablespoons of mix.

Country Hearth Coffee Mix

1/4 cup granulated sugar
3 tablespoons powdered coffee creamer
3 tablespoons instant nonfat dry milk
1 tablespoon instant coffee granules
2 teaspoons unsweetened cocoa powder
1/4 teaspoon ground cinnamon
1/8 teaspoon ground nutmeg
Dash of salt

Place all ingredients in a food processor or blender and process until consistency of a fine powder. Place in a small zipper-type bag. Recipe makes 4 - 5 servings.

To prepare: Microwave 3/4 cup of water on high power for 1 to 1-1/2 minutes or until hot. Stir in 2 to 2-1/2 tablespoons of mix.

Desserts
in a Mug
Gift Ideas

Gift Mugs:

To give these mixes as a gift, line the inside of a mug (one that matches your theme—birthday, get well, thank you, Christmas, Valentine's Day, etc.) with colorful tissue paper.

Place one bag of mix inside. Write the cooking instructions on a small tag and attach it to the handle of the mug using ribbon or raffia. Or write the instructions on a recipe card and tuck it inside the mug with the mix.

If the recipe calls for a container of vegetables or fruit, simply place the container in the bottom of the mug and the mix on top.

Using ribbon or raffia, you can also attach a decorative item that is appropriate to the mix (such as a small wire whisk, wooden spoon or cinnamon stick).

Birthday Cake Gift Mug

Place a bag of yellow or chocolate cake mix and a bag of chocolate frosting mix in a mug that has been lined with colorful tissue paper.

You can use a "Birthday" mug if you like. Tuck a few birthday candles inside with the bags of mixes.

Write the cooking instructions for the cake mix and frosting mix on a small tag. Attach it to the mug handle using bright-colored curling ribbon. Or write the instructions on a recipe card and place it inside the mug.

To add extra pizzazz to your gift, buy a small Mylar "Happy Birthday" balloon attached to a stick and insert it into the mug.

"Thanks a Latte" Gift Mug

Place a bag of Chai Tea Latte Mix in a mug that has been lined with colorful tissue paper.

Using ribbon or raffia, attach a tag with the cooking instructions.

From poster board or construction paper, cut a small sign (about 1-1/2" X 2-1/2") and write "Thanks a Latte" on it using colorful markers. You can also print a small label on your computer and cut it out.

Glue or tape the sign to a wooden skewer or drinking straw and insert into mug.

"You're a Peach" Gift Mug

Place a bag of Peach Scone Mix, Peach Cobbler Mix or Peach Crisp Mix (along with a snack-size container of peaches) in a mug, lined with colorful tissue paper.

Using ribbon or raffia, attach a tag with the cooking instructions to the handle or write the instructions on a recipe card and tuck inside the mug.

From card stock, cut a small sign (about 1-1/2" X 2-1/2") and write "You're a Peach!" on it using colorful markers.

Or use your computer to design a sign using clip art, as shown in the photo, and cut out.

Glue or tape the sign to a wooden skewer or drinking straw and insert into the mug.

Other Occasions For Gift Mugs

Desserts-in-a-mug mixes make great gifts for many occasions. Just a few ideas are listed below:

- "Get Well Soon": include one or two bags of hot cocoa mix

- "A+ Teacher": include a bag of Apple Nut Bread mix or Apple Pie mix

- "Welcome to the Neighborhood": include a bag of Blueberry-Lemon Coffee Cake mix

- "You're Hot Stuff!": include a bag of Hot Fudge Cake Mix

- "Happy Valentine's Day": include a bag of Chocolate Covered Cherry Fudge Mix

- "Merry Christmas": include a bag of White Chocolate Cranberry Candy Mix or Mulled Tea Mix

Follow the directions for the "Thanks a Latte" gift mug and make a sign for the appropriate message to insert inside your mug. Don't forget to attach a tag with the instructions for preparing the mix.

Coffee-Lover's Gift Basket

Line a small basket with colorful paper shred or a fabric napkin. Place a mug inside the basket.

Choose several mixes made with coffee, such as Chocolate Mocha Brownie Mix, Cappuccino Chocolate Chip Muffin Mix, Coffee Banana Scone Mix, Caramel Coffee Mix and Country Hearth Coffee Mix.

Place each mix in the center of a 12-14" square of fabric (you can also use fabric napkins) or colorful tissue paper. Gather the corners of the square together around the mix and secure with ribbon, jute or raffia.

Write the cooking instructions for each mix on a small tag and attach with ribbon or raffia. Place the bundled mixes in the basket around the mug.

Chocolate-Lover's Gift Basket

Follow the instructions for the Coffee-Lover's Gift Basket, but use several chocolate cake, candy or beverage mixes to include in your chocolate-lover's gift basket, such as German Chocolate Cake Mix, Chocolate Cherry Brownie Mix, Chocolate Mint Fudge and Amaretto Hot Cocoa.

"Afternoon Tea" Gift Basket

Follow the instructions for the Coffee-Lover's Gift Basket, but use breakfast treat and beverage mixes for a delectable afternoon tea party for one.

You might include Cranberry Oat Scone Mix, Lemon Walnut Scone Mix, Apple Nut Bread Mix, Chai Tea Latte Mix or Hot Mulled Tea Mix.

"Sweetie Pie" Mug or Gift Basket

For a mug gift, place one pie mix in a mug lined with colorful tissue paper. Using ribbon or raffia, attach a tag with cooking instructions to the handle. From card stock, cut a small sign (about 1-1/2" X 2-1/2") and write "You're a Sweetie Pie!" on it using colorful markers. You can also design a sign on your computer using clip art or copy the sign below onto card stock and cut it out. Color the design with markers if you like, and glue it to a wooden skewer or drinking straw, then insert into the mug.

For a gift basket, line a small basket with colorful paper shred or a fabric napkin. Place a mug inside the basket. Choose several pie mixes to include in your "sweetie pie" gift basket. Place each mix in the center of a 12-14" square of fabric (you can also use fabric napkins) or colorful tissue paper. Gather the corners of the square together around the mix and secure with ribbon or raffia.

Write the cooking instructions for each mix on a small tag and attach with ribbon or raffia. Place the bundled mixes in the basket around the mug. Insert the "sweetie pie" sign on a stick.

Recipe Index

Dessert Mixes

Breakfast Treats

Coffee Cakes:
  Blueberry-Lemon, 66
  Cinnamon Crunch, 67
  Mango, 71
  Mocha, 72
  Orange Fudge, 68
  Pear, 69
  Piña Colada, 70

Fruit Breads:
  Amaretto Peach, 74
  Apple Nut, 75
  Banana Nut, 76
  Cherry Pecan, 77
  Cranberry Orange, 78

Muffins:
  Applesauce Oat, 80
  Blueberry White
    Chocolate, 81
  Cappuccino Chocolate
    Chip, 82
  Pineapple, 83
  Sweet Potato, 84

Scones:
  Chocolate Chunk, 92
  Christmas, 91
  Coffee Banana, 86
  Cranberry Oat, 87
  Gingerbread Raisin, 88
  Lemon Walnut, 89
  Peach, 90

Hot Beverage Mixes

Coffee:
  Caramel, 102
  Country Hearth, 104
  Gingerbread, 103
  Mocha Cappuccino, 102

Hot Chocolate:
  Amaretto, 100
  Malted, 100
  Mexican, 98
  Orange Spice, 99
  Snowman Soup, 101

Tea:
  Chai Tea Latte, 94
  Chocolate Tea, 95
  Friendship Tea, 97
  Hot Mulled Tea, 96

Vanilla Sugar, 6

About the Author

Gloria Hander Lyons has channeled 30 years of training and hands-on experience in the areas of art, interior decorating, crafting and event planning into writing creative how-to books. Her books cover a wide range of topics including decorating your home, cooking, planning weddings and tea parties, crafting and self publishing.

She has designed original needlework and craft projects featured in magazines, including *Better Homes and Gardens, McCall's, Country Handcrafts* and *Crafts.*

Gloria also teaches interior decorating and self publishing classes at her local community college.

Visit her website for free craft ideas, decorating and event planning tips and taste-tempting recipes:

www.BlueSagePress.com

Ordering Information

To order additional copies of this book, send check or money order payable to **Gloria Lyons** at:

 Blue Sage Press
48 Borondo Pines
La Marque, TX 77568

Cost is $9.95 for this edition (U.S. Currency)
Shipping & Handling Charges: $3.50 for the first book and $1.50 for each additional book shipped to the same address in the U.S.A. Texas residents add 8.25% sales tax to total order amount.

To pay by credit card or get a complete list of books, visit our website: www.BlueSagePress.com

Other Books by Gloria Hander Lyons

- *Easy Microwave Desserts in a Mug for Kids*
- *If Teapots Could Talk: Fun Ideas for Tea Parties*
- *A Taste of Memories: Comforting Foods From Our Past*
- *Quick Gifts From the Kitchen: No Cooking Required*
- *40 Favorite Impossible Pies: Main Dishes & Desserts*
- *Quick & Easy Sandwich Wraps*
- *The Secret Ingredient: Tasty Recipes with an Unusual Twist*
- *Hand Over the Chocolate and No One Gets Hurt! The Chocolate-Lover's Cookbook*
- *A Taste of Lavender: Delectable Treats with an Exotic Floral Flavor*
- *Lavender Sensations: Fragrant Herbs for Home & Bath*
- *Designs That Sell: How To Make Your Home Show Better & Sell Faster*
- *Ten Common Decorating Mistakes & How to Avoid Them*
- *Decorating Basics: For Men Only!*
- *Self-Publishing On a Budget: A Do-It-All-Yourself Guide*
- *Flamingos, Poodle Skirts & Red Hots: Creative Theme Party Ideas*
- *The Super Bride's Guide for Dodging Wedding Pitfalls*
- *Kiss My Grits, Sugar: Southern Humor with a Side of Tasty Fixin's*
- *Pearls of Wisdom For Creating A Joyful Life*
- *What's Up With That? Humorous Short Stories About Life in Modern-Day America*

For a complete list of all our creative how-to books, visit our website: www.BlueSagePress.com or write to request a book catalog: Blue Sage Press, 48 Borondo Pines, La Marque, TX 77568